Human

Praise for Daniel Corrie

Daniel Corrie's poetry is scripture for our troubled Anthropocene Era. Patiently distilled, sometimes over many years, Corrie's poems are deeply imaginative, clear, sonically rich, stylistically ambitious, original, and significantly meaningful.... Corrie's poetry is an unusual melding of largeness, vividness, dreaminess, and the meditative.... Corrie's is a poetry of consequence: his work is deeply committed to the creation of artistic means of addressing our time's environmental degradations, including climate change and species extinctions. Yet, while Corrie's poetry without apology engages such concerns of the world, his poetry extends beyond green poetics. Corrie's poetry often is ritualistically incantatory and of dream imagination.

—William Wright,
writing in *Terrain.org*

...[Daniel Corrie's] books are a gift. The poems they contain represent the best talents of what might be called the *placed poet*. They are specific and regional while also sweeping and universal: "Pine shape before me / stood for me, risen analogical— / meaning-bearer—" Their scope extends beyond the standard celebrations and warnings of "eco-poetry" since they are concerned with the health of the world along with the health of the human soul.... These poems are patient, studied, felt, transformative, and mythic....

—John Saad,
writing in *The Birmingham Poetry Review*

Human

Poems

Daniel Corrie

Iris Press Chapbook Series

Copyright © 2018 by Daniel Corrie

All rights reserved. No portion of this book may be reproduced in any form or by any means, including electronic storage and retrieval systems, without explicit, prior written permission of the author, except for brief passages excerpted for review and critical purposes.

ISBN: 978-1-60454-507-4

Cover artwork: *Flora*, digital image by Selwyn Rodda (selwynrodda.com).

Page 1: *Lost in a Sky Full of Stars,* photograph by Benjamin Davies (www.benjamindavies.co).

Page 10: *Edmund's Snaketail*, photograph by Giff Beaton (giffbeaton.com).

Page 13: *Longleaf Pine Sapling on Fire*, photograph by Brady Beck (bradybeckphotography.com).

Page 37: Middlemarch *in Wiregrass and Longleaf Pine Needles*, photograph by Glenn Josey (glennjosey.com).

Page 40: *Smoky Sunburst*, photograph by Brady Beck (bradybeckphotography.com).

Book Design: Robert B. Cumming, Jr.

Iris Publishing Group, Inc
www.irisbooks.com

Acknowledgments

Poems from this book appeared in the following journals:

Hudson Review: "The Lives in Novels"

Terrain.org: "The Ancient Surge of Stars and Night Opens As All Being's Single Bloom" and "Words of Time, Book of Fire"

•

"Dragonfly: Edmund's Snaketail" appeared in *A Literary Field Guide to Southern Appalachia*, University of Georgia Press, edited by Rose McLarney and Laura-Gray Street.

•

*The author thanks Robert Cumming
and Beto Cumming.*

For Thomas Carper,
in memory

Contents

Dragonfly: Edmund's Snaketail • 11

Words of Time, Book of Fire

    i. *Riddle of Sun* • 14
    ii. *Riddle of Pages* • 18
    iii. *Riddle of a World* • 24
    iv. *Riddle of Sparks* • 30
    v. *Riddle of Moments* • 33

The Lives in Novels • 38

The Ancient Surge of Stars and Night Opens As All Being's Single Bloom

    i. *Emerge* • 41
    ii. *Augury* • 42
    iii. *Self* • 43
    iv. *The Beauty of the Earth* • 44

It had no doubt become incredible that Zeus and the other gods were living on top of Mount Olympus. You could go to the top and find no trace of them.

—Walter T. Stace

Through consciousness, a pile of rocks can become the memorable Mount Alten which one has climbed and upon which one almost perished.

—E. D. Klemke

…the Earth is a biospiritual planet….

—Thomas Berry

All landscape contains the potential world.

—John Hay

Dragonfly: Edmund's Snaketail

> *This species is currently known only from six counties.... It was thought extinct in the 1970s and 1980s....*
> —Giff Beaton

You wing to perch in the tree's crown,
to still as jeweled yellow-green.

Your wings are panes overlooking
current's clear and tireless pouring.

Through spring into the summer's onset,
you haunt greens' spectrum of woods

leveling to foothill's chill seams
riffling over erosions of rocks.

River's shallows ripple through rocks
for you to claim, to scud patrolling

your glinting stint of territory.
Mosquitoes' plague and fate of flies,

your hunger scans through leaves.
Your globes of eyes veer out from eras

of genes' lines past your reckoning,
launching the rush of flight to the kill.

An arrow's shaft, you fly to hunt
the targets of your four wings' course.

A phallic shaft in flight, you sheer
through air to wings arcing up

from rock's island. You clinch her.
She arches her clubbed tail to you,

pair bending to one wheel of two of you.
You circle eggs shuddering from her,

not knowing a man's name names you.
Among human numbers, you don't know

the nearing of zero. Caught in sight,
your gleaming is beauty in sunlight

over waters where instincts know
streams, rocks and trees' heights.

For now, April carries your rarity's
facet of time you are. For now, you are

a jeweled valediction, a living brooch
you give to a branch, jeweling time.

Words of Time, Book of Fire

i. *Riddle of Sun*

Fat roots that fucked deep
will shrivel.

From drought's
dry earth, tall weight will fall.

A pine's risen branching's
once-green, once-supple
needles will parch,

brown litter fallen to crumble
when touched.

Wings will find sky's flyways
that upraised eyes might target

to recognize in passing
as a tanager's red wings
will blaze, flickering from

another instinct-guided return
to April's branch.

Like sea ice thawing, television glass
floats its dark surface

until a pushed button flashes it
into glimpses
of vistas of white

ice ridges crumbling
into slushy sea.

Through polar wastes, forests
rose then died and froze,

as they would rise again
in warming sunlight.

Glaciers bled their freshets
streaming down from summits,

as they would bleed away again
in warming sunlight.

Ocean spilled over plains,
as waves would spill

again in warming sunlight.

Eyes will cut to follow then lose

red's departing through green
flushing from branches' seasons

of diurnal survival.

The blood-red feathers remember
through their color,

red's memory veering as veins
into rivers, clearing to the air

of flyways' courses.

Two wings will rise beating
among flocks of wings.

One by one, each caught in itself,

each bird flies
into instincts' beckonings.

Skies of days revolve away
into night sky's return,

horizon rounding
the width of a world,
measuring time's hours.

A night's clouds will clear
into the great distances

of the great night

always continuing
to spread, widening farther

into time's sheer continuing.

The great night continues
to become itself,

to carry all spirals
of stars' fire, of stardust,

of cyclopean clouds
and rubble.

The great night ferries
the drift of debris.

Great time is the chronicle
of the drift of debris.

In a forest's night,

leaf embers rise to drift,

sparks widening
into wildfire widening

into becoming itself.

A wakening began
wakening itself toward more

than impulse, strangeness
opening through savannas
of strangeness,

spreading to seed
night's continents with luminous
blooms of cities

and day's tall stems of stacks
belching their blooms
of gray haze.

The gritty drift opens

as smoke rose hazing
from carnage's campaigns,

demarcations of borders
lost in the flaming

of maps shriveling into embers,

each column climbing, billowing
mirrored in eyes

to blear after eyes
have shifted away,

smoke shredding into the sky

of clouds' metamorphoses

and the sun.

ii. Riddle of Pages

Time opens its night

littered with
its phase of stars.

The book drifts open

forever hinging
toward forever's

last chapter of embers.

The book of time slams open.
Sudden, blown pages

lash, whipping into blurring.

Coal-red wings of pages float.

Each page's eon passes, flashing

as each wingbeat flashes, passing.

The book offers
its pages' blank oblivions.

Each page accepts
a ledgered lettering.

Glimpsed mantra after mantra
inscribes itself, to shimmer

through pages' charring.

Sutras smolder into smoke.

Each sky of each page darkens

shriveling into black,
receding beyond the words'

incandescent letters floating

into nights' constellations.

The electric freshet blazes a way.

Dream-steps waken

into finding their way, following
the line of meaning's swift,
luminous runnel.

The synaptic, coursing descent
radiant as lava
is the edge that guides
the footholds' steep ascent.

The words speak themselves

as burning branches speak
their consumption, crackling
into recitation,

heard in illumination.

The oneiric gaze of upraised eyes
sweeps out through stars

to the farthest rondures
opening through all

of night's eon-skull,

steps entering starless dark's
void through rock's skull

of a cavern's cool,
sunless echo.

The ocher-painted walls
had been washed by torchlight
flickering through

skull-cradled thoughts.

A transformation persisted
winnowing itself

perpetually provisional

into swarming thoughts' feverish
flaming of naming.

A going was guiding itself
climbing somewhere

swept with glimpses
of a vista's distances
flickering through cloudcover's rifts.

Up through itself,
scouting beyond itself,

a going would scale
clinging to a cliff face

up through itself, to debouch
beyond itself.

Mind would ascend

a mountain it would begin to feel
itself becoming,

maps of rivers
cascading, sparkling into rivers.

To emerge from time
to see through time—

through mind, to see—

red fire floating
in its bloating glare,

senescent sun oblivious
of oceans steamed away
from arid beds' horizons.

To emerge from time,
to peer out through time—

brief minds would come to see

out through years counted
by a few sun-tethered worlds'

billioning circles, finally to wheel

through fire's expansion,

worlds scattering as cinders' flocks.

The turning page withers, collapsing.

The page crumbles
into ashes of archives'

measured and studied astronomies.

Smoke's rise undulates, scroll
snaking in wind.

Smoke chronicles a pyre billowing
into dying away

beyond the long reign
of bacteria swarming
and churning

into joining and becoming
the burning.

Sun will consume stones

imprinted with what were once
wind-stirred fronds

and pinecones scattered
on ancient sun-dappled ground.

Sun's lucence will consume

remnant stones shaped
from the shifting guises that flickered

to shards of hungering, searching
ape-shapes and man-shapes

sunken, locked under deepening
earth's layers and weather's
vagaries of ages
of ice, lightning and baking drought.

Mind would come to see the sun
floating in its laws.

Mind would come to see clouds ruled
by sky's intricate laws.

The littered letters
brand themselves into the pages

hissing words
smoking into disappearing.

There in the page, a mantra
is another spring migration
of a tanager
glinting to a branch.

There, winter forgets itself
through ice cliffs collapsing.

There, a sutra is sun's
glimmer over a river

of traffic inching over miles

of a highway's baking asphalt.

iii. Riddle of a World

Empty cavern of a skull

had held a night of bison running
across cavern walls,

all held deep
in unheld night.

Some fragments will be dug
and lifted into sunlight,
carefully brushed
of earth and numbered.

Other rubble will remain
incarnations gone, like memories

unrecoverable through layers
lost in layers.

Parchment chars.

Smoke rises washing
into eddies, as waters eddy.

Rivers know nothing
of lives ending on banks

declared to be borders.

Maps' paper yellows.
Maps metastasize,

browning into blotches
knowing nothing

of ink's delineations.

A river's rush fights
its war against rocks,

until carving its strength
as a hill's arid scar.

Drought abrades green
scoured into sand.

Rivers offer their waters

to the conquering sun.

The photograph holds

a monk in last gesture,
cross-legged on asphalt

in the orange of a robe,

in the orange of gasoline's
aura of flames.

The moments gleam
through an image past pain
of one life's sum

in fire's orange lens.

Flames' sinews ripple.

Sparked pistons slam.

Asphalt's scroll spills
toward desert's sinking sun.

A human skull hovers
in flames. It floats

in sunburned skin
of bicep's ink,
leather-chapped thighs

hugging gas tank's
paint-sprayed slash
of meteoric flames.

Circle mirrors circle.

Vortex twins vortex.

The two tires blur
locked in chassis.

The two wheels whirl

caught as in curse
of pursuit.

Caught in one course,

one wheel races never
to catch the other,

as one wheel will never
evade the other.

They pass roaring

toward somewhere.

Unearthed, ore's fierce

incandescence pooled

cupped in cauldrons
to be poured and forged.

Steel wheels clattered
down steel tracks,

steel car following steel car

heaped, trailing windrush's
wake of black dust

to snake across plains
under night skies' drifts

of cauls of clouds
eclipsing constellations.

Unremembered forests
darkened into ore,

finally torn from mountains'
soil renamed overburden,

to be reborn in fire.

Pines sun-hungered
to open into themselves.

Like messengers, pines
stood in their waiting.

Finally, a time ripened

into a choosing of time—

time of the possible
times that might be chosen.

Sun-summoned beauty hungered
to become itself.

Pines climbed, sun-sung paeans.

Out from the smoke
of the burning page—

Out from great time's drift—

Out from all of blind time,
first eyes budded

to later mind opening

into a time for seeing
sunfall's world—

to see it—to know it—

to be it—to keep it—

until voices within voices
finally ripple through flocks

departing through sky—

voices of messengers.

Blowing through sky,
a hiving of words

will whine away, farther
from words

forgetting words—*I plucked*

*the gleaming apple
from a branch*—

The page wilts, warping
the imprinted words

of the ineffable fable—

*then I saw the branch
struck brittle*

*as the tree of knowledge
creaked and cracked*

in sunglare as it fell—

The scattering of words

will flock as birds chattering

into the mute distances.

Mosquitoes' swarms will whine

lassoing into wind-whine's
swarms of sand

calming to pages' ashes
drifting down.

    iv.   Riddle of Sparks

Foreheads raised
in Wednesday's rite
will wear the black of ashes.

Voices will take flight

choiring within walls
lifting windows'

sun-brightened spectrums.

Panes' puzzle pieces join.
They glow, coloring

the numinous scenes
of a savior's sacrificial life

and of a mute angelic visitant
hovering on wings—

sun's illuminated world

eclipsed past colored glass.

In dusk, the spectrum dims.

A book's black and red
scriptures imprint the white

of pages' allegories
of the good and of

the eclipsing of the good.

Seed heads rose

to sway in wind
through fallen columns

of gods' ruined temples.

Color of blood, like drops
fallen in sun-warmed grasses,

would open into blooms' red

of ratany, cardinal flower,
bee balm, crimson clover.

A pulse will throb. It will repeat

through a wrist's red warmth
of blood's passing.

Being's mantra will repeat.

The mantra of being's
question will echo,

echo's repetitions dwindling,

dimming as words'
black ink sinks

into a page's black charring—

what lived as you?

what lived as you?

Hand will let go of hand.

Form will depart from form,

the ashes of permanence

floating through aftermath.

The great book's pages
will shrink away to sparks

showering through darkness,

darkening into darkness.

It will burn away.

It will be the teeming
phase of stars

entering the end of stars

cooling and crumbling.

Beyond time's youth
of the great, bright spirals,

residue will float, unraveled.

Darkness into darkness,

atoms will flock away

into separating.

Atoms will drift farther

from other atoms,

detritus parting

in unfelt cold

of the ultimate night—

of the conquering night—

v. Riddle of Moments

Viridescence opened

promising all leaves
into opening.

Time summoned

in a moment in the sheen
of a temperate sun,

into the feeling of days
becoming themselves.

In all of great time,

the self would cobble
its redoubt of selfhood

at its decades' borders.

A line crosses an empty field
of the white of a page,

line of words extending into words,

line of sky's invisible flyway
wings follow into exodus,

line following into generations
following into generations,

line of viridescence

becoming all leaves
ever to open.

Meaning's mantras would quiet

until silent as ashes floating.

In the page
of the ineffable fable,

two wings return in spring
through flocks of wings,

sunlight warming morning air
to sift through leaves,

aeolian breath whispering

of the scattered triumphs—

to see it—to be it—

Oblivious sunlight

reached down from sky, bestowing
what would become

the verities

of viridescence—

to live as you—

to have lived as you—

What comes to appear, seeming
the good or the true—

what comes to seem to be
meaning and meant—

whispers, trailing into rustling
aeolian through a life.

The lived decades might find
the invisible flyway

through the verities.

A year follows years' flyway
circling sun's radiance.

Borne by, born into

great, oblivious time,

the moments open
into becoming themselves.

Feeling might find the flyway
through the moments

of the meant.

SUNSET AND SUNRISE

Her finely-touched spirit had still its fine issues, though they were not widely visible. Her full nature, like that river of which Cyrus broke the strength, spent itself in channels which had no great name on the earth. But the effect of her being on those around her was incalculably diffusive: for the growing good of the world is partly dependent on unhistoric acts; and that things are not so ill with you and me as they might have been, is half owing to the number who lived faithfully a hidden life, and rest in unvisited tombs.

THE END

The Lives in Novels

>...*thinking of an action as if it*
>*were eternally repeated....*
>—Genevieve Lloyd

i.

Open the book. It is where time is held.
You read the story, as their lives repeat
where their world opens to another world.

Where their book's pages open to your light,
your eyes look down. It's a familiar story.
See their returning lives which they forgot

imprinted in typography. They hurry
toward their same decisions. Swept in being
themselves again, they feel their seconds carry

their lifetimes forward, all their minutes fleeing
into an unchanged plot you've known before.
You've read the book, and you remember seeing

the lines of syllables advancing over
the page, to colonize a void's white field.
The hours begin, again, to disappear.

ii.

Their destinies find form, indelible.
Captured in ink, no moment ever passes.
Raskolnikov remains in some swift hell

descending as an ax that never ceases
falling in words. Words scatter down the page
like meaning stilling into fractured pieces.

Emma Bovary haunts her story's cage
of paragraphs, where she breathlessly chases
rewards remote beyond each chapter's age.

Line follows line, where Dorothea traces
the forking paths of choices, as though to find
and mend the world. The alphabets of guesses

combine to sentences, as hours extend
into some chronicle where time is still
rustling through the lives the hours pretend.

The Ancient Surge of Stars and Night Opens As All Being's Single Bloom

i. *Emerge*

Orange of oriole
will flash as aureole
of afterimage.

Pines will stand
in orange aureole,
each a shrine of fire.

Words will mist in winter,
flocks chattering
to swirl to sky
to clear like breath in air.

Blown snow will lift
drifting cloudily
to pollen's gold,
to twist to sand's blind lash.

Like faces, sunflowers
turn toward the far fire.

It is the fire floating,
centering the circle
of their world's course.

Through murky depths
of uterine night,
all stars swirl out, colloidal,
to rupture and kindle.

As icicles melt
in sun's brightening,
raised megaliths will melt
in time's night.

Wrecked trucks will rust
under a bright
ceiling of waves.

ii. *Augury*

You would walk listening

in passing beneath
final branches' glaring aura.

Tides will shift seeping
through marsh grass,
as sand's hot blaze will drain
glittering through fingers.

Dunes will drift burying
urns of cars, deeper
than sun's punishment.

Wind's dunes will shimmer,
unearthing the colors
of cars' pitted paint.

Like ebb tide's surf,
tree lines will ebb.

Like leaves' sheltered shade,
plumage's browns
will hide through leaves
of forests receding.

Wings' sudden flurry
will be wings vanishing
in the rites of flight.

You would walk listening

in entering the hearing
of the minutes'
last song of the last
bird of its kind.

You might be who waits
in the moment of a trill
stilling into silence,

opening into echoes.

iii. Self

You will echo as you walk
under branches, listening.

Dull plumage of veery
mirrors shade, blending.

Its song's repetitions
pronounce living beauty.

You will falter, following
past each narrow tomorrow.

The speech of echoes
will repeat the few words
for you to follow
like steppingstones.

Your entered moments
will hover like mist
over a river's
deafening fall and crash.

You will hear wind's tide
flood through the tall pines
as aeolian orisons.

You will hear
your voice finding
the words of your orison
like the span of horizon.

Your seeing will dawn
through benisons of branches.

You will be a bearer
of what will be,

as you echo. You will echo.

You will be the bearer
of what you will be,

as you echo. You will echo.

iv. *The Beauty of the Earth*

Meaning, abandoned
to the middens, will lift
from your starless abyss

as you echo. You will echo.

Echoing through rondure
in your skull's inner mirror,
sky's blue will know you

as you echo. You will echo.

You will hear the moment
that is your life sung
by a bird taking wing

as you echo. You will echo.

Wind will bear wildfire's
bright seeds, sparking
into bright wildflowers

as you echo. You will echo.

You will feel your spine rise
to echo the towering
pine among pines

as you echo. You will echo.

Your autumn will hold
how goldenrod glows
yellowing into hallowing

as you echo. You will echo.

When you hear the roar
of the course of the river,
you will follow its echoes

as you echo. You will echo.

Left behind you, its waters
will be a wake's shimmer
that anyone might follow

called by echoes, who will echo.

Daniel Corrie's first full-length book of poems is near completion. Chapbooks of his poetry include *For the Future* (Iris Press) and *Words, World* (Blue Horse Press). His poems have appeared in *The American Scholar, Birmingham Poetry Review, Greensboro Review, Hudson Review, Image, Kenyon Review, Measure, Missouri Review, The Nation, New Criterion, Shenandoah, Southern Review, Southwest Review, Terrain.org, Virginia Quarterly Review,* with poems selected for five anthologies and for *Verse Daily*. One of his poems received the first-place 2011 Morton Marr Poetry Prize. He and his wife live on their farm in rural Georgia.

www.ingramcontent.com/pod-product-compliance
Lightning Source LLC
LaVergne TN
LVHW010309070426
835510LV00025B/3417